Nasmyth, Wilson of Manchester built few industrial locomotives but two of them, built for Astley and Tyldesley collieries in Lancashire, were amongst the finest ever produced in Britain. 17 inch (432 mm) 0-8-0T 'Maden' was built in 1910 (works number 918) and had Walschaerts valve gear and the refinement of outside-admission piston valves. Note the abundance of wooden-bodied wagons in this 1955 picture.

INDUSTRIAL STEAM LOCOMOTIVES

Geoffrey Hayes

Shire Publications Ltd

CONTENTS

Printed in Great Britain by C. I. Thomas & Sons (Haverfordwest) Ltd, Press Buildings, Merlins Bridge, Haverfordwest, Dyfed.

British Library Cataloguing in Publication Data available.

ACKNOWLEDGEMENTS
The author wishes to acknowledge the assistance given by members of the Industrial Railway Society in the preparation of the text and in providing illustrations. Messrs E. R. Etherington, R. E. West, D. L. Chatfield, J. A. Peden and F. Smith have all rendered valuable assistance. Thanks are also due to Roy Etherington, Roger West and my wife, Naomi, for reading the text most carefully and making many useful suggestions for its improvement. Photographs are acknowledged as follows: D. L. Chatfield, pages 18, 29; K. J. Cooper Collection, courtesy of the Industrial Railway Society, page 25 (lower); Grant Ross, page 27; Frank Smith, page 7. All the rest are by the author, with acknowledgement to the National Museums of Scotland for permission to photograph 'Wylam Dilly'.

Cover: *Many Scottish-built industrial steam locomotives had a striking family likeness and a good number of the founders of thses firms had started their careers with Andrew Barclay of Kilmarnock. Prestongrange number 7 was built in 1914 by Grant, Ritchie of Kilmarnock (works number 536) for the Lothian Coal Company and is a 15 inch 0-4-2ST. This type on the standard gauge is almost a Scottish phenomenon. Number 7 is preserved at the Scottish Mining Museum, Prestongrange.*
Below: *Built for the 2 foot 3 inch (686 mm) gauge Corris Railway by the Hughes Locomotive and Tramway Engine Works, Loughborough, in 1878 (works number 323), number 3 started life as a 7 inch (178 mm) 0-4-0ST. In 1900, to improve stability, she was converted to an 0-4-2ST by the Falcon Engine and Car Works, which had succeeded Hughes. Although built for a line that carried passengers, number 3 was a standard Hughes industrial type built in several gauges. Named 'Sir Haydn', number 3 now works on the Talyllyn Railway. The Falcon Works became Brush Electrical Engineering.*

The oldest steam locomotives in the world are 'Wylam Dilly' and 'Puffing Billy' built by William Hedley for Wylam Colliery in 1813. 'Wylam Dilly' (preserved in the Royal Museum of Scotland, Edinburgh) has a return flue boiler. Because of rail breakages, it was later rebuilt with eight wheels, to spread the weight, and was converted back to four wheels when the railway was relaid with wrought iron edge rails. The track gauge is 5 feet (1524 mm).

INTRODUCTION

The steam railway locomotive is a British invention and the first in the world ran in South Wales in 1803. Its inventor was Richard Trevithick, a genius and a giant of a Cornishman. This locomotive was intended for heavy haulage over a relatively short distance in the service of an industry. Over the next twenty years the coal-mining industry became a considerable user of the steam locomotive. Their success led to the development of the country-wide railway system carrying both goods and passengers. At first there was little difference between the locomotives used at the coal mines and those of the new main line railways but, from about 1830 onwards, the different requirements led to a divergence of locomotive types.

The use of locomotives to serve industry became widespread from the 1850s. There were several reasons for this. Demand for coal, iron and manufactured goods was increasing enormously; the main line railways had rapidly developed, providing quick and easy transport to nearly all parts of Britain and the tank locomotive had been invented which carried its own supply of fuel and water. Until then all locomotives had carried their supplies in one or sometimes two separate vehicles or tenders, making a long and rather unwieldy machine. The new design made a compact motive power unit ideal for short-distance haulage.

By the end of the nineteenth century the industrial steam locomotive had reached its final form and afterwards there was improvement only in details. This contrasts with the constant search for improved efficiency in main line locomotives. On short and heavy hauls there is little scope for fuel economy. Reliability and ease of maintenance are the most important features. The final industrial locomotives of the 1950s hardly differed from those of 1900 except for a very few notable examples.

3

In contrast to the main line railways, very few industrial concerns built their own locomotives. These were supplied by locomotive-building firms located in most industrial areas with the general exception of the Black Country and South Wales. There were, however, three main centres where builders of industrial locomotives were concentrated — Bristol, Leeds and Kilmarnock. Each builder produced locomotives of distinctive outline and the products of Bristol and Kilmarnock were as different in appearance as the locomotives of the Great Western and London and North Eastern railways.

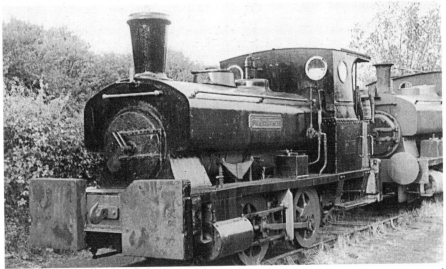

Andrew Barclay of Kilmarnock built industrial steam locomotives for the best part of a century and all had a distinctive, easily recognised outline. 'Swanscombe' used to work at Thurrock Chalk and Whiting in Essex and is a 12 inch (305 mm) 0-4-0ST built in 1891 (works number 699). She is now preserved at Quainton Road. Note the huge wood-block buffers, a feature of many Scottish-built industrial locomotives. A Barclay 0-4-0ST of 1925 peeps into the picture behind.

The British Aluminium Company at Burntisland in Fife used this 10 inch (254 mm) 0-4-0ST, BAC number 2, built by Peckett and Sons, Bristol, in 1915 (works number 1376). She is now preserved on the Lochty Private Railway. The bell-mouthed dome cover houses the dome and the safety valves as well. Note the wooden-bodied wagon typical of those used in the heyday of the industrial steam locomotive.

4

Industrial steam locomotives were few in Ireland. Number 3 of Guinness's Brewery in Dublin is a Hudswell, Clarke 15 inch (381 mm) 0-4-0ST of 1918 (works number 1152). Being Irish, the track gauge is 5 feet 3 inches (1600 mm). The skirt over the wheels was a protection required by the government on locomotives working along the public highway. Number 3 is now preserved at the Belfast and County Down Railway Trust.

INDUSTRIAL RAILWAYS

No one knows when the first rails were laid to ease the passage of wheeled vehicles or wagons. Such railways, or tramroads as they were usually known, were in use in the seventeenth century and by the end of the eighteenth century had become quite extensive in the new and booming industrial areas of Britain. They were used to carry heavy materials such as stone, coal and metalliferous ores from the place where they were quarried or mined to the nearest navigable waterway or the sea. In those days, water provided the only means of bulk transport over long distances.

The success of these early lines led to the development of the country-wide network of main line railways from 1825 onwards. At this point the industrial and main line railways began to go separate ways. Parliament conferred great powers and also great obligations upon the main line railways. Where a mine or quarry lay some way off the route of a main line, it was easier, quicker and cheaper for the owners to construct their own line over their own land or by arrangement over their neighbours' lands to the nearest point on the main line system.

Rails in the very early days were of wood, cast iron or even stone. Cast iron was mostly used and these rails were often of L-shape, the upstand keeping the plain wheels of the wagons on the track. Some rails were different in shape, looking like the letter I, and the wheels of the wagons had to be flanged to keep them on the line. These were known as edge rails. When the early locomotives were introduced, their weight frequently broke the brittle cast iron. It was not until a cheap method was developed of producing wrought iron edge rails, which, being malleable, did not break easily, that locomotives were successfully used. A great benefit of these new edge rails was that friction between rail and wheel was greatly reduced compared with the old L-shaped cast iron tram rails.

In 1848 Parliament decreed that the gauge, that is the distance between the rails, of all main line railways in Britain should be 4 feet 8½ inches (1435 mm) except in the case of very minor lines, where narrower gauges could be used if sanctioned by Parliament. For convenience the majority of industrial railways used this standard gauge, but there were

Some very small locomotives were used on the lightly laid and temporary tracks in quarries and on public works contracts. 'Pixie' was used by Devon County Council in a roadstone quarry. She is a 2 foot (610 mm) gauge, 6 inch (152 mm) 0-4-0ST built by Kerr, Stuart of Stoke-on-Trent in 1922 (works number 4260) with Hackworth valve gear and now operates on the Leighton Buzzard Narrow Gauge Railway.

many odd gauges. It may be thought that standard gauge was itself an odd measurement, as indeed it was, originating in the coalfields of north-east England and perpetuated by George Stephenson. Ireland adopted a much more logical gauge of 5 feet 3 inches (1600 mm). Many of the peculiar gauges came about when

The Hunslet Engine Company built a series of 15 inch (381 mm) 0-6-0T locomotives for the Manchester Ship Canal Company. Number 22, built in 1902 (works number 778), is at Partington Coaling Basin in 1955. An identical locomotive, formerly MSC number 14, is preserved on the Severn Valley Railway.

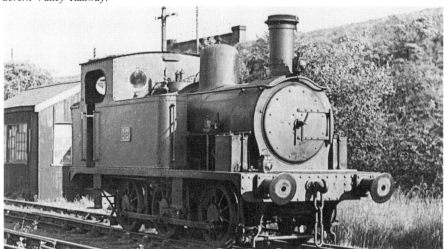

edge rails were substituted for tram rails. For a concern having a large number of wagons it was easier to change the wagon wheels from plain to flanged and lay the new rails to suit the wagons. These odd gauges survived a long time where there was no need to transfer wagons between main line and industrial railways.

In the second half of the nineteenth century very many main line railways were built and also many public works were undertaken, such as the construction of reservoirs for water supply to cities. The requirement for moving large quantities of earth and bringing construction materials to the site led to another type of industrial railway, the temporary or contractor's railway. This type of railway was even used in more modern times in the construction of new roads and bypasses, being replaced only when the bulldozer, heavy dump truck and other massive earth-shifting machinery came into use. The largest ever contract using temporary railways in Britain was the construction of the Manchester Ship Canal.

When the first main line railways were built they were regarded almost as public highways and industrial concerns such as collieries were able to operate their own trains with their own locomotives over them. This system of working led to chaos and was soon stopped but in the colliery districts of the north of England this relic of early days continued until the 1960s. A legacy of this practice was the private-owner wagon: a colliery, factory or any other concern would run their own wagons on the main line system to carry their products and raw materials. At the beginning of the Second World War this practice ceased as all railway rolling stock came under government control but up to that time there were half a million private-owner wagons running on the railways of Britain. After a lapse of many years, private-owner wagons are again running on the main line railway and to an increasing extent.

Until about 1960 there were many industrial railways in Britain, ranging from a few hundred yards of track to large systems with more than a hundred track miles . One very large system was the permanent railway operated by the

A carefully posed 1908 scene at a Wigan colliery. Large numbers of wooden-bodied private-owner wagons are visible, lettered 'Wigan Coal & Iron Cy. Limited'. The locomotive is 'Manton', a 16 inch (406 mm) 0-6-0ST recently built by the company. The headgear, engine house and tall chimney belong to Alexandra Pit and in the background are the smaller buildings and headgear of Lindsay number 3 Pit.

Manchester Ship Canal number 59 was a 15½ inch (394 mm) 0-6-0T built by Hudswell, Clarke of Leeds in 1913 (works number 1046) and had long side tanks and inside cylinders. Identical locomotives numbers 67 and 70 are preserved on the Keighley and Worth Valley Railway and the East Lancashire Railway.

Manchester Ship Canal Company. The reason for such railways was that until the middle of the twentieth century nearly all of the nation's goods was carried by rail.

The method of working goods traffic on industrial railways, and on the main line railways too, changed little in a hundred and fifty years. By the mid twentieth century the method had long become archaic. Most wagons were con-structed largely of wood and capacity was small, averaging only 10 or 12 tons. Train working was loose-coupled unbraked. Wagons were coupled together with three-link chains which hung slack when the buffers were touching. Wagon brakes could be applied only by someone standing on the ground. The only way of stopping a train was by applying the brakes on the locomotive. A few indust-

A colliery near Wigan in 1955. The locomotive is the 16 inch (406mm) 0-6-0ST 'Balcarres', built by the Wigan Coal and Iron Company in 1892. A similar locomotive is preserved at Steamtown, Carnforth. Much in evidence are wooden-bodied wagons. The man is the shunter carrying his shunting pole used for coupling and uncoupling wagons.

rial railways used a guard's brake van on the trains as on the main lines but the overall braking effort was small compared with the weight of the trains. On falling gradients the train could easily overpower the locomotive's brakes plus those of a brake van and it was necessary to stop at the top of a gradient and walk along the train applying the wagons' brakes before descending. Overall speeds were therefore very low: the national average for main line goods trains was about 7 mph (11 km/h), and no figures were ever attempted for industrial railways.

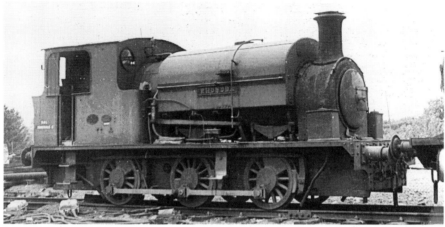

Corby steelworks used Manning, Wardle of Leeds 16 inch (406 mm) 0-6-0ST locomotives in the iron ore quarries serving the works and gave them the names of Welsh towns. 'Rhondda' was built in 1921 (works number 2010) and was eventually transferred to Harlaxton quarries. She is now preserved at Caister Castle near Great Yarmouth.

The original designs of E. B. Wilson gave locomotives built by Manning, Wardle of Leeds a distinctive outline recognisable from the 1850s until 1929, when the firm closed. 'Warwickshire' is a 14 inch (357 mm) 0-6-0ST built in 1926 (works number 2047) and worked at a Rugby cement works. She is preserved on the Severn Valley Railway.

INVENTORS AND BUILDERS

Richard Trevithick was the first to apply strong steam, as it was then known, to driving a steam engine. Instead of using steam at just above atmospheric pressure and relying on a vacuum produced by condensing the exhaust steam to give a useful effort on the piston, he took the revolutionary step of using steam at two or three times atmospheric pressure. At this pressure a condenser was not needed and the engine could exhaust straight into the air. With steam at such a pressure, a small engine was able to do the work of a much larger low-pressure engine. Trevithick was soon experimenting with his high-pressure engine as a locomotive,

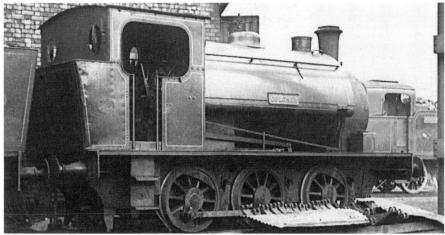

The 15 inch (381 mm) 0-6-0ST 'Colonel' built by the Hunslet Engine Company, Leeds, in 1927 (works number 1459) for Atherton Collieries in Lancashire. Hunslet called this type of locomotive the Airedale class and the first one of the class is preserved on the Embsay Steam Railway.

'Ring Haw', a 16 inch (406 mm) 0-6-0ST built by the Hunslet Engine Company, Leeds, in 1940 (works number 1982) for Nassington iron ore quarries. This locomotive is now preserved on the North Norfolk Railway.

Stewarts and Lloyds, the steelmakers, ordered eight identical 18 inch (457 mm) 0-6-0ST locomotives from the Hunslet Engine Company, Leeds, in 1940 for use at Corby. In 1941 they were requisitioned by the government for various steelworks, iron ore quarries and the Army. 'Gunby' (works number 2413) is seen at Harlaxton quarries and has since been preserved on the Stour Valley Railway.

During the Second World War many shunting locomotives were needed at Army depots and elsewhere. Hunslet modified their design of 18 inch (457 mm) 0-6-0ST for Stewarts and Lloyds and produced the 'Austerity' shunter. Several locomotive manufacturers built them and Hunslet carried on after the war. Over five hundred were eventually built, a record for one type of industrial locomotive. This is Army number 197 'Sapper', built by Hunslet in 1953 (works number 3797). It now operates on the Kent and East Sussex Railway as 'Northiam'.

both on the ordinary road and on rail.

In 1803, Trevithick designed his first locomotive for practical use on rails, albeit tram rails, and set it to work on the Pen-y-Daren Tramway in South Wales. Unfortunately, Trevithick soon faded from the locomotive scene and it was left to others, mainly in the north of England, to develop the steam locomotive. By 1815, Blenkinsop, Hedley and George Stephenson had all built successful locomotives for use on colliery railways. Remarkably, two of Hedley's locomotives survive, both of them built in 1813 and remaining at work until 1862. It was George Stephenson, though, who developed the steam locomotive into a form which could run at speed over long distances.

By the late 1840s the main line railways, now well established, needed light locomotives to work the branch lines they

With the appropriate name of 'Thomas', this 16 inch (406 mm) 0-6-0T in light blue livery worked at the British Sugar Corporation factory at Peterborough and is now preserved on the Nene Valley Railway. It was built by Hudswell, Clarke of Leeds in 1948 (works number 1800).

Slough Estates number 5 is a 15 inch (381 mm) 0-6-0ST which served the large industrial estate at Slough. It is now preserved on the Embsay Steam Railway. It was built by Hudswell, Clarke of Leeds in 1939 (works number 1709) with outside cylinders and a saddle tank, in contrast to those with inside cylinders and side tanks built for the Manchester Ship Canal.

had laid to act as feeders to the trunk main lines. In 1848, George England at his works in the Old Kent Road, London, and W. Bridges Adams at Bow, East London, produced tank locomotives which carried their own supply of coal and water instead of in a separate tender. At the Railway Foundry, Leeds, E. B. Wilson was building tank locomotives for collieries by 1855. His business folded in 1858 but not before another firm, Manning, Wardle, had set up next door. They took over many of E. B. Wilson's designs. Two more firms, Hudswell, Clarke and the Hunslet Engine Company, were established in Leeds within the next six years and were building locomotives for use in industry. A much older Leeds firm,

The railway serving Pye Hill colliery in Nottinghamshire passed under a very low bridge and all the locomotives had to be cut down to clear it. The Hunslet Engine Company built 0-4-0ST number 11 (works number 1493) for the colliery in 1925, and the locomotive is now preserved on the Market Bosworth Light Railway.

The iron ore quarries of the East Midlands were served by many miles of industrial railways. Locomotives were often named after local villages. 'Stainby', seen here at Buckminster quarries, Leicestershire, was an Andrew Barclay 15 inch (381 mm) 0-6-0ST built in 1951 (works number 2313). An identical locomotive is preserved at the Rutland Railway Museum, Cottesmore, and another at Quainton Road, Aylesbury.

Kitson and Company, who concentrated largely on main line locomotives for home and abroad, also developed a range of industrial locomotives. Also in Leeds, John Fowler, better known as a maker of steam ploughing tackle and road engines, built considerable numbers of industrial locomotives, mainly for export.

Andrew Barclay started a general en-gineering business in Kilmarnock in 1842 and in 1847 built a new workshop, the Caledonia Works. In 1859 he started building locomotives for the local collieries and ironworks. Later, several other firms which also built industrial locomotives were established in the town. Despite a hand to mouth financial exist-ence for forty years from 1859, Andrew

In 1918, during the First World War, Andrew Barclay brought out a design of narrow-gauge 0-4-0WT locomotives based on German practice. Works number 1431 was built for the 2 feet (610 mm) gauge line at Calshot seaplane base, Southampton. In 1953 it was regauged to 2 feet 3 inches (686 mm) for use on the Talyllyn Railway, where it became number 6, 'Douglas'. Typical European features are the Belpaire firebox and Walschaerts valve gear. Note the small wagons, common on slate-carrying and many other narrow-gauge industrial railways, which could be shunted by hand.

Barclay has outlived all the other firms and occasionally builds locomotives today, although with diesel engines.

As well as Leeds and Kilmarnock, a major industrial locomotive-building centre was the city of Bristol. The firm of Fox, Walker was established in the early 1860s and for some twenty years built mainly industrial locomotives. Falling on hard times, the business closed but the

This hefty 16 inch (406 mm) 0-6-0ST still manages to retain the Bristol look. Built by Peckett and Sons in 1939 (works number 1970) for the Ashington Coal Company, the locomotive is now preserved on the North Norfolk Railway. Now named 'John D. Hammer', it is also a memorial to the late engineer of that railway.

Scottish builders had almost a monopoly of crane locomotives and this 0-4-0 has other not so usual features as well — inside cylinders and side tanks. Number 6 was built by Neilson and Company of Glasgow in 1890 (works number 4004) and worked at Hodbarrow Haematite Mines near Barrow-in-Furness. Her job was loading and hauling timber from the stockyard to the mines.

The large colliery railway systems in the north of England used 0-6-2T locomotives, some of which were bought second-hand from the main line companies. The Stoke-on-Trent works of the North Staffordshire Railway built number 2 in 1923. She then became London Midland and Scottish Railway number 2271 and was sold in 1937 to Manchester Collieries Limited, who named her 'Princess'. She is now preserved as NSR number 2 at Chatterley Whitfield Mining Museum, Stoke-on-Trent.

Ungated level crossings were quite common on industrial railways. A train en route from St George's limestone quarries to the main line sidings at Foryd Junction, Clwyd, trundles across a country road. The locomotive is 'Margaret', a 14 inch (356 mm) 0-6-0ST built by the Avonside Engine Company, Bristol, in 1923 (works number 1923). A similar locomotive is preserved at Steamport, Southport.

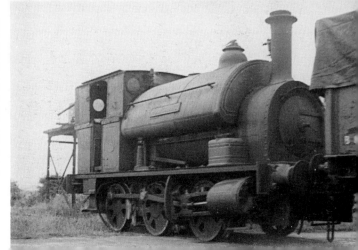

In the 1920s the Sentinel Waggon Works of Shrewsbury developed a successful light shunting locomotive based on their steam lorries and tractors. 'Craven' was built for Craven Brothers of Reddish, near Stockport, and was later disposed of to Rugby Portland Cement Company at Totternhoe limestone quarries in Bedfordshire. The vertical boiler is in the cab and the high-speed engine under the bonnet at the front. Between cab and engine is the water tank. 'Craven' was a 100 horsepower (75 kw) type built in 1953 (works number 9556). Similar locomotives are preserved at Bo'ness and Summerlee.

works was bought by Thomas Peckett, who, as the firm Peckett and Sons, quickly became a major builder of industrial locomotives, developing the original Fox, Walker designs. The firm continued in business until the general cessation of steam locomotive building and closed in the early 1960s after an unsuccessful venture into building diesel locomotives. In 1889 Edwin Walker managed to restart locomotive building in Bristol as the Avonside Engine Company, which con-

Black, Hawthorn of Gateshead were prolific builders of industrial locomotives but had gone out of business by 1900. 'Holwell number 3' is a 12 inch (305 mm) 0-4-0ST built in 1873 (works number 266), which worked at Holwell Ironworks in Leicestershire. She migrated to various iron ore quarries and finally to Wirksworth limestone quarries in Derbyshire. Note the old-fashioned arrangement of the dome on the firebox. She is preserved on the Tanfield Railway.

'Singapore' is a 12 inch (305 mm) 0-4-0ST of the neat design made by Hawthorn, Leslie of Newcastle upon Tyne. She was built for the Admiralty in 1936 (works number 3865), who sent her to Singapore Dockyard. Captured by the Japanese in February 1942, she was in enemy hands until August 1945. She was returned to Britain in 1952. The dents in saddle tank and cab were made by bullets. She is preserved at the Rutland Railway Museum.

For the iron ore quarries of the Rockingham Forest in Northamptonshire, which supplied the massive Corby steelworks, Robert Stephenson and Hawthorn designed a powerful 0-6-0ST with 18 inch (457 mm) inside cylinders. Number 60, 'Jupiter', was built in 1950 (works number 7671) and eventually worked at Buckminster quarries in Leicestershire. She is now preserved on the Colne Valley Railway.

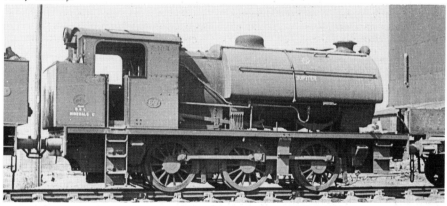

tinued until about 1930, when the works closed with the goodwill being taken over by Hunslet of Leeds.

As may be expected, Tyneside, with its George Stephenson connection, was well to the fore in locomotive building. In the last quarter of the nineteenth century Black, Hawthorn of Gateshead built considerable numbers of industrial locomotives but by 1900 the firm had gone out of business. Their successors, Chapman and Furneaux, lasted only a few years, leaving but one firm, Hawthorn Leslie of Newcastle, producing industrial locomotives in quantity. The famous Robert Stephenson Company, together with old-established locomotive builders in Lancashire and Glasgow, concentrated on

Aveling and Porter of Rochester made three types of locomotive, all based on their road engine designs. A total of 130 were built, the first in 1862 and the last in 1926. 'Sir Vincent' is one of the third type produced and was built in 1917 (works number 8800). Mounted on top of the boiler is a two-cylinder compound engine. Steam from the boiler is admitted to a small high-pressure cylinder and then exhausts to a larger low-pressure cylinder to do further work before exhausting to the chimney. 'Sir Vincent' is now preserved at Hollycombe. Examples of the other two types of Aveling and Porter locomotives are preserved at the London Transport Museum and on the Bluebell Railway.

Herbert Garratt designed an articulated locomotive which was produced in great numbers and in very large sizes by Beyer, Peacock of Manchester. Some of these locomotives are still at work in Africa. Four locomotives with the wheel arrangement 0-4-0+0-4-0 were built for industrial use in Britain. The locomotives were powerful and could traverse sharp curves. 'Number 3', built in 1931 (works number 6729), worked at Sneyd Colliery, Stoke-on-Trent. An identical locomotive is preserved at Bressingham Live Steam Museum.

main line locomotives, particularly for export.

Birmingham and the Black Country were remarkably devoid of locomotive builders, the nearest being W. G. Bagnall of Stafford and Kerr, Stuart of Stoke-on-Trent.

There were many firms who built only a handful of locomotives, particularly in Scotland, and very few industrial concerns who built their own, notably the Wigan Coal and Iron Company.

The industrial depression of the 1920s and 1930s saw many well known locomotive-building firms disappear, a process which has continued ever since, except for a brief respite during the Second World War and just after. Very few builders of locomotives of any type now exist in Britain.

Built for the Steel Company of Wales by Bagnall of Stafford in 1951 (works number 2996), 'Victor' was one of three identical locomotives with all possible labour-saving devices — roller bearings, a firegrate which could be rocked and dropped to clear ashes and clinker, and a hopper ashpan from which ash could be dumped in seconds. With 18 inch (457 mm) cylinders having inside-admission piston valves and Walschaerts valve gear, these 0-6-0ST locomotives were formidable haulers. 'Victor' is seen at Minehead on the West Somerset Railway but now operates on the Strathspey Railway.

Kerr, Stuart of Stoke-on-Trent built ten 17 inch (432 mm) 0-6-0T locomotives in 1917 for the Inland Waterways and Docks Commission. With larger boilers than usual and very robust construction, they were excellent machines. 'Francis' (works number 3068) was sold to Bridgewater Collieries in 1919 and was in service until 1967. Unfortunately none of these fine locomotives has survived into preservation. Note that the locomotive has a Belpaire firebox.

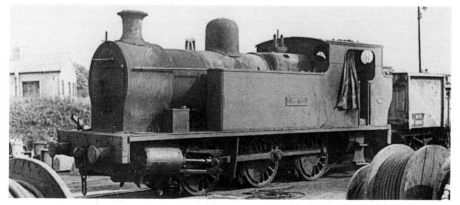

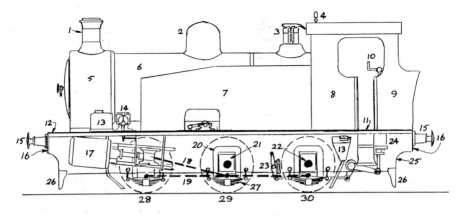

Diagram of a 16 inch 0-6-0 side-tank locomotive, showing the parts of a steam locomotive. 1 Chimney, 2 Dome cover, 3 Ramsbottom safety valves, 4 Whistle, 5 Smokebox, 6 Boiler, 7 Side tank, 8 Cab, 9 Coal bunker, 10 Hand brake, 11 Footplate and cab steps, 12 Running plate, 13 Sandbox, 14 Mechanical lubricator for cylinders, 15 Buffers, 16 Buffer beams, 17 Cylinder, 18 Connecting rod, 19 Coupling rod, 20 Horn (axlebox guide), 21 Axle box, 22 Axle, 23 Brake block and hanger, 24 Steam brake cylinder, 25 Frame, 26 Guard iron, 27 Spring, 28 Leading driving wheel, 29 Driving wheel, 30 Trailing driving wheel.

HOW A STEAM LOCOMOTIVE WORKS

The steam locomotive is a machine for converting heat contained in fuel into useful work. It does not do it very well and the industrial steam locomotive in particular is very inefficient. Hardly more than 5 per cent of the heat in the fuel, and often less, is converted into useful work. The first stage in the process is to burn fuel and pass the released heat into water which then evaporates into steam. This is done in the boiler. As the boiler is a closed vessel, the formation of steam causes pressure to build up. Steam at pressure is passed from the boiler to the cylinders, of which there are usually two, controlled by a regulator which is operated by the driver. The cylinders are each fitted with a sliding piston which the steam forces along, rather like blowing down the end of a bicycle pump. Through a system of rods the effort is transmitted to the wheels, and from the wheels and their axles this effort is passed through the frames to the drawbar. Fixed to the drawbar is a hook to which a train of wagons can be attached by chain.

To keep the wheels rotating, the pistons have to move to and fro in the cylinders continuously. So that the pistons are pushed in the correct sequence, the steam has to be admitted and exhausted or released at the right time. This is usually done in industrial locomotives by a slide valve, which is a kind of shoe that is moved backwards and forwards over slots or ports connected to each end of the cylinder. The slide valve and ports are in a box, the steam chest, into which the steam is piped after passing through the regulator. The slide valves obtain their motion from the valve gear, which is usually driven by off-centre discs, eccentrics, fixed on the driving axle. The valve gear also provides the means of making the locomotive go forwards or backwards and is connected by rod and links to the reversing lever in the driver's cab. This lever also provides another means of controlling the flow of steam into the cylinders. Moving the lever from the forward or backward full-gear position towards the central mid-gear position reduces the amount of movement transmitted to the slide valves. This cuts off the steam earlier in the piston's travel or stroke. Steam has expansive properties

20

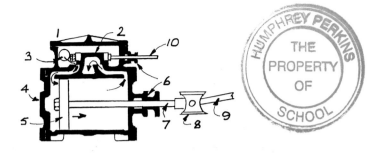

Diagram of a cylinder and slide valve. Steam from the boiler works in the cylinders, and the power developed is largely dependent on the size of the cylinders. The diameter is known as the bore and the distance the piston travels is the stroke. Dimensions were always measured in inches and typical dimensions are 14 inches bore and 20 inches stroke, 15 inches by 22 inches, 16 inches by 24 inches, 18 inches by 26 inches. The numbers indicate the various parts. 1 Steam chest, 2 Slide valve, 3 Steam inlet, 4 Cylinder cover, 5 Piston, 6 Glands, 7 Piston rod, 8 Crosshead, 9 Connecting rod, 10 Valve spindle. The passages connecting the steam chest to the cylinder are known as ports.

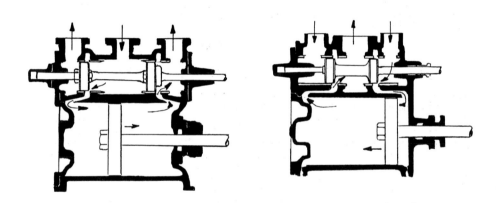

Diagrams of a cylinder and piston valve, (left) with inside admission, and (right) with outside admission. Piston valves were seldom fitted to the cylinders of industrial locomotives although they gave a better steam flow and needed less effort to move than slide valves. They were, however, much more costly to make. On some piston valves steam from the boiler flowed past the outer ends of the valves — outside admission; on others the steam flowed through the centre or inside part of the valve — inside admission.

and, although cut off, continues to push the piston with diminishing but still useful force, thereby saving steam. Many main line locomotives could do their work with a cut-off at 25 per cent of the piston stroke but industrial locomotives very seldom worked at less than 50 per cent

cut-off.

A few industrial locomotives had piston valves instead of slide valves. These perform exactly the same function as slide valves but are bobbin-shaped and, accordingly, the steam chest is tubular. Piston valves were common on main line

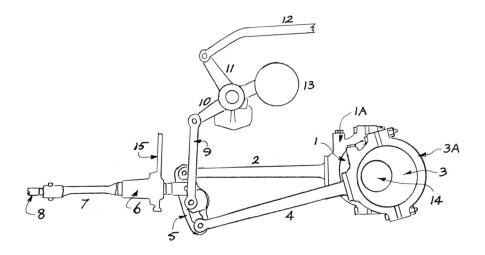

Diagram of Stephenson valve gear, which was the most commonly used on British industrial locomotives. In the diagram it is shown in full forward gear. 1 Forward eccentric sheave, 1a Forward eccentric strap, 2 Forward eccentric rod, 3 Backward eccentric sheave, 3a Backward eccentric strap, 4 Backward eccentric rod, 5 Expansion link, 6 Valve spindle guide, 7 Intermediate valve spindle, 8 Valve spindle, 9 Lifting link, 10 Lifting arm, 11 Reversing arm, 12 Reversing rod (to reversing lever in cab), 13 Balance weight, 14 Driving axle, 15 Motion plate.

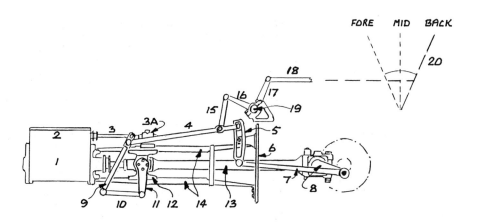

Diagram of Walschaerts valve gear, which, although widely used on modern main line locomotives, was not so common on industrial locomotives. It is shown in full backward gear. 1 Cylinder, 2 Steam chest, 3 Valve spindle, 3a Valve spindle guide, 4 Radius rod, 5 Slotted link, 6 Motion plate, 7 Eccentric rod, 8 Eccentric crank, 9 Combination lever, 10 Union link, 11 Crosshead arm, 12 Crosshead, 13 Connecting rod, 14 Slide bars, 15 Lifting link, 16 Lifting arm, 17 Reversing arm, 18 Reversing rod, 19 Weigh shaft, 20 Reversing lever.

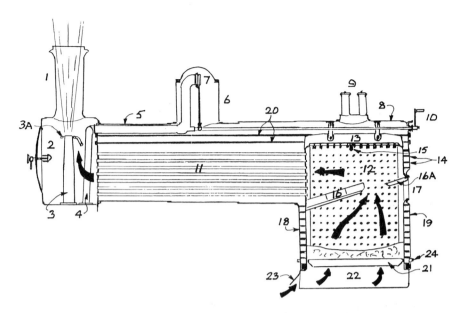

Diagram of a locomotive boiler. A locomotive-type boiler is a complex assembly and most of the vital parts are seen only by those who make or repair them. The numbers indicate most of the principal parts. 1 Chimney, 2 Smokebox, 3, 3a, Blast pipe and blower, 4 Steam pipe, 5 Boiler barrel, 6 Dome, 7 Regulator valve, 8 Outer firebox, 9 Pop safety valves, 10 Regulator handle, 11 Tubes, 12 Firebox, 13 Roofing bar and sling stays, 14 Stays, 15 Fusible plug, 16, 16a Brick arch and deflector plate (not fitted in small boilers), 17 Firedoor, 18 Throat plate, 19 Firebox back plate, 20 Longitudinal stays, 21 Firegrate, 22 Ashpan, 23 Damper, 24 Washout plug.

locomotives as they allowed a better flow of steam into and out of the cylinders at high speeds.

The most common type of valve gear was Stephenson's, introduced by George Stephenson in 1843. It was rarely seen by the casual observer, usually being tucked away out of sight between the locomotive's frames. Another valve gear was invented by a Belgian engineer, E. Walschaerts, and this was always visible as it was placed outside the locomotive's wheels. There were other but less common valve gears. Hackworth's valve gear can be seen on the Kerr, Stuart locomotives working on the Talyllyn Railway and the Leighton Buzzard Narrow Gauge Railway.

Boilers on the very early locomotives were very simple. A cylindrical vessel contained a single large tube. At one end of the tube was the fire and at the other was the chimney. To increase the surface area of tube in contact with the water — heating surface — some boilers had the tube arranged in a U-shape — the return flue boiler. This form of boiler was not efficient and a lot of heat went uselessly up the chimney. It was quite common for early locomotives to stop frequently from lack of steam. George Stephenson overcame this problem in the *Rocket*, built in 1829. He used a boiler invented by a Frenchman, M. Seguin, in 1827 which had a very large heating surface. The fire was placed in a large box surrounded by water, the firebox, from which the flames and hot gases were passed through the cylindrical part of the boiler, the boiler barrel, by a large number of small tubes which were also entirely surrounded by water, before being allowed to escape up the chimney.

The principle of passing exhaust steam from the cylinders through a nozzle — the blast pipe — and directing the resultant jet up the chimney, to create a fierce draught on the fire and make it burn with intense heat, had been applied very early in locomotive history. Applied to the

23

boiler on the *Rocket*, plenty of steam was produced, ensuring its success. Henceforth this type of boiler was known as the locomotive-type boiler.

Most locomotive boilers have a dome where the regulator is fitted so that steam is collected for the cylinders as far above the water level as possible. All steam engines work best with dry steam and water in the cylinders can cause serious damage. Essential fittings on the boiler are the safety valves, which release steam if the pressure becomes too high, the pressure gauge, which indicates the pressure of steam in the boiler, and the water gauge showing the level of water in the boiler. The water gauge is a glass tube fitted between two cocks on the firebox backplate. The water should always be visible in the glass tube. If it disappears in the bottom of the gauge the water is very low and overheating of the firebox will occur, often with disastrous explosive consequences. As a final line of defence against the consequences of low water, a lead-filled fusible plug is fitted in the roof

or crown sheet of the firebox. Should the temperature rise because the water is low, the plug melts and the steam and water which deluge into the firebox at least partially quench the fire.

Water at too high a level in the boiler will be carried into the cylinders, possibly causing damage. However, between the upper and lower safe limits of water level there is a considerable volume of water. Water has a tremendous capacity for storing heat and this is the reason why an industrial locomotive could perform such apparent prodigies of haulage. The harder a locomotive is worked the more steam is used, all of which is exhausted through the blast pipe. This increases the draught, causing the fire to burn more fiercely and so produce more steam. There is, however, a limit to what can be produced. If the demand for steam exceeds this limit steam pressure in the boiler begins to fall. The effect of this is to release heat from the water and this causes some of it to turn into steam, giving an extra supply over and above what is being produced by the heat of the fire alone. This super-effort can only be maintained whilst there is a safe level of water in the boiler and steam pressure remains high enough to pull the train. Having made the effort, the locomotive has to rest while the water level and steam pressure are recovered.

As water evaporates into steam the boiler has to be replenished and this is done by the injectors. These are devices which use steam pressure and a system of nozzles to force the water into the boiler against the pressure in the boiler. To keep the fire burning when the locomotive is stationary or running with steam shut off, the blower is used. This is a steam jet directed up the chimney and taking steam directly from the boiler.

Footplate view of a small Peckett 0-4-0ST locomotive. Visible are the sliding firedoors, the water gauges and regulator handle. Also visible is the large nut securing a longitudinal stay and the screw-in washout plugs. The round heads belong to the firebox stays. On top of the firebox are the wheels controlling the blower valve, injector steam valves (one wheel missing) and steam brake valve. Just visible is the whistle handle and the pressure-gauge shut-off cock.

Bagnall of Stafford were well known for their 6 inch (152 mm) 0-4-0ST locomotives fitted with launch-type boilers and intended for use on lightly laid and temporary tracks. 'Pixie' is 2 foot gauge (610 mm), built in 1919 (works number 2090), and worked for some years at Cranford iron ore quarries removing the gannister which overlaid the iron ore beds. Gannister is a valuable material used for making blast-furnace linings. 'Pixie' has outside cylinders and Walschaerts valve gear and now operates on the Cadeby Light Railway.

De Winton of Caernarfon supplied a great deal of machinery to the North Wales slate quarries. Their 0-4-0 locomotives with vertical boilers stood the test of time. 'Chaloner' was built in 1877 and worked on the 2 foot (610 mm) gauge lines at Pen-yr-Orsedd slate quarry. She now operates in preservation on the Leighton Buzzard Narrow Gauge Railway. Other De Winton locomotives may be seen at the Narrow Gauge Railway Museum, Tywyn, and at Gloddfa Ganol, Blaenau Ffestiniog.

Fireless locomotives were a speciality of Andrew Barclay and works number 2243, built in 1948, worked at Laporte Chemicals. It is now preserved at Quainton Road, Aylesbury. Features of the fireless locomotive were the obvious lack of a chimney and cylinders located under the cab. Exhaust steam was directed up a pipe at the rear of the cab.

Although the locomotive boiler is a marvellous producer of steam, it is difficult and costly to make and requires careful maintenance. The large flat surfaces of the firebox have to be strengthened with hundreds of stays. To accommodate these and the tubes and the rivets which hold the boiler plates together, an enormous number of holes is necessary, all of which are a potential source of leakage in service. A locomotive boiler under construction appears more like a gigantic colander than a vessel for holding steam and boiling water under pressure. To reduce the difficulty and cost of construction, some locomotive builders used the launch-type boiler on small locomotives intended for light duties. The firebox was circular and did not require stays. It was not as good a steam producer as the locomotive boiler but it was adequate for light work. Simpler still was the vertical boiler, which stood upright, though it was even less effective than the launch-type boiler. Nevertheless it was used on some small locomotives. A good example operates on the Leighton Buzzard Narrow Gauge Railway.

For use in factories where there was a great risk of fire, or where absolute cleanliness was essential, locomotive designers used the heat-storing property of water to the limit and produced locomotives which had no fire at all — the fireless locomotive. In place of the boiler, a large well insulated cylindrical tank was used, three-quarters full of water. Charged with steam at high pressure from an external source, the locomotive could perform several hours work using up the heat stored in the water.

To stop the train, brake blocks are forced against the locomotive's wheels. Small or old locomotives had hand brakes which multiplied the effort provided by the driver's muscles by a screw thread and linkage. Later and larger locomotives used steam acting on a piston — steam brakes — to press the brake blocks against the wheels, but they also have hand brakes for emergency and for parking.

Apart from the effort which can be exerted by steam on the pistons, a limiting factor in starting a train is the grip or adhesion of the wheels on the rails. Even more important, it is also a limiting factor when stopping. To get the maximum amount of adhesion, industrial locomotives had all their wheels coupled together wherever possible so that the whole weight of the locomotive was available. Wet or greasy rails seriously reduce the grip of the wheels and, to assist starting and stopping, locomotives carry a supply of sand in boxes with pipes leading down to the rails. By operating a handle in the cab the driver can allow sand to be trickled on to the rails.

LOCOMOTIVE TYPES

It was important that users of locomotives should know precisely what they were buying from the builders and also that builders should be able to interpret customers' requirements. The system adopted was to state the diameter or bore of the cylinders, as this defined the power, the arrangement of the wheels and the position of the water tank. Apart from the very early ones, few industrial locomotives had separate tenders. Water was carried in several ways: in a tank wrapped over the top of the boiler (saddle tank); in tanks along each side of the boiler (side tanks); between the frames underneath the boiler (well tank); in tanks slung on the shoulders of the boiler (pannier tank). These positions were usually abbreviated to ST, T, WT and PT. A shorthand way of describing locomotives was thus developed. A locomotive with 16 inch (406 mm) diameter cylinders, six wheels all coupled together and a saddle tank was described as 16 inch 0-6-0ST and everyone knew what was meant.

Cylinders could be fitted either between the frames under the smokebox (inside cylinders), or outside the frames, again directly below the smokebox (outside cylinders). Most outside-cylinder industrial locomotives still had their steam

Many industrial locomotives were exported, especially to the British colonies, even by small makers. Alexander Shanks of Arbroath was best known as a manufacturer of lawn mowers but in the 1870s was making a few small industrial locomotives. Destined for the tropics, 'Tat' has a spark-arrester chimney for wood burning and a canopy over the footplate to protect the driver from the sun. She is an 0-4-0ST with about 9 inch (229 mm) cylinders and has been manhandled on a rickety temporary track out of the works into the street. On the other side of the street, opposite the works, is the Dundee to Aberdeen railway and with the aid of further temporary track 'Tat' was manhandled through the fence, on to the railway line and then probably towed to Dundee docks for shipment.

chests and valve gear inside but there were some which had the whole assembly outside. It is an interesting exercise when looking at industrial locomotives to determine whether they have inside cylinders, outside cylinders with inside steam chests and valve gear, or outside cylinders with steam chests and valve gear outside as well. The position of the cylinders depended on the whim of the designer and the wish of the customer.

The different wheel arrangements all had their particular uses and these are as follows:

0-4-0. A very widely used type on all gauges of railway. With a short wheelbase, it could travel round sharp curves. The type was usually built with saddle tank and outside cylinders. Other varieties were less common.

0-4-2. This type could negotiate curves almost as sharp as the 0-4-0. The rear carrying wheels were fitted in a special truck which allowed them to move from side to side. Used quite extensively on narrow gauges, the type was rare on standard gauge except in Scotland. Side and saddle tanks were used and outside cylinders were in the majority. The 0-4-2 type was used where a larger boiler and more coal and water capacity was required than could be fitted on an 0-4-0 but the line on which it worked had sharp curves. Some 0-4-0 locomotives were converted to 0-4-2 to improve stability.

0-6-0. A very popular type used wherever line curvature permitted. A larger boiler could be fitted than on an 0-4-0 and the ride was much better. For equal power, the weight carried by each pair of wheels was also less. The type was built in all possible configurations of side, saddle and pannier tanks and cylinder position. There were also some well-tank locomotives and in north-east England some tender engines of this type were used at collieries.

0-6-2. Developed from the 0-6-0, this type was quite large and rather rare, used mainly on some large colliery railway systems. Several main line locomotives were purchased second-hand for use on these systems. The majority had inside cylinders and side tanks. A few locomotives of this type with outside cylinders were used on the narrow-gauge system at Kemsley Mills, Kent.

0-8-0. In contrast to the continent of Europe, where the type was widely used, only three were built for use in Britain.

0-4-0+0-4-0. An articulated locomotive designed by H. Garratt and built by Beyer, Peacock of Manchester. The design allowed a large and powerful locomotive to traverse sharp curves and run on lightly laid track. Only four were built for industrial use in Britain.

Compared with the main line railways, there were very few types of locomotive in industrial use and indeed 0-4-0 and 0-6-0 far outnumbered all the rest. As may be expected in a total number of locomotives running into thousands, there were a few examples of other wheel arrangements. The main reason for the adoption of these rare types was that they had been bought cheaply second-hand.

Until about 1900 there was little difference in basic design between industrial and main line locomotives. From that date the increasing requirements of speed and loads made the main line railways seek improved performance and fuel economy in their locomotives. There is little scope for economy in a locomotive performing short, heavy hauls and the state of the art in 1900 was quite adequate for this type of duty. Even the main line railways continued to use basic Victorian designs for their shunting and short-distance goods locomotives.

There were a number of special designs of industrial locomotive. The simplest variant was the cut-down locomotive. Some locomotives had to work in very low places, such as under gas-making retorts, and were very much reduced in height. Others worked on lines which had originally been horse-worked, with over-line bridges to suit the height of a horse. It was cheaper to obtain low-height locomotives than to alter bridges.

The conventional steam locomotive is heavy; it also takes a long time to raise steam in the mornings. Numerous attempts were made to reduce the weight and cost of locomotives and the time needed for raising steam. Two distinctive designs were produced by firms whose main production was steam road vehicles. Aveling and Porter of Rochester, Kent, produced a locomotive design based on their traction engines and road rollers. A quick-running engine was mounted on top of a locomotive-type boiler and the drive was transmitted to the wheels by gearing, or by gearing and chains. The very smooth turning movement at the wheels (like bottom gear on a car), as opposed to the four large impulses of a conventional locomotive, meant that a lighter locomotive could start the same load without slipping. Speed was very low, however, and the reduced weight was not beneficial for stopping the train.

A more sophisticated design was produced by the Sentinel Waggon Works of Shrewsbury, Shropshire. Their special design of vertical boiler could raise steam in a very short time and this supplied a fast-running vertical engine which was fully enclosed, like the engine of a car. Power was transmitted to the wheels by means of a gearbox and chains. This was a very good design and quite widely used. However, it required good-quality, almost smokeless, coal and very clean soft water.

Some industries, particularly shipbuilders and large foundries, required heavy items such as large steel plates and castings to be loaded into wagons at a stockyard, transported for some distance within the works and then unloaded. For these duties an odd-looking locomotive was designed — the crane locomotive. Usually an 0-4-0 side-tank locomotive was used as the basis for the design, with a crane mounted over the middle of the boiler or sometimes over the smokebox. In the latter case the chimney was used as the pivot. The crane unit had small steam engines which provided the movements for lifting and slewing. A few of these locomotives have survived into preservation and can be seen at Foxfield, Staffordshire; Bressingham, Norfolk; Butterley and Dinting, Derbyshire; and on the East Somerset Railway, West Cranmore. Scottish locomotive builders, including those in Glasgow, made this type of locomotive something of a speciality.

Introduced by the Stephensons in the 1840s, the long-boiler 0-6-0 locomotive could negotiate sharp curves. National Coal Board (now British Coal) number 41 is an 0-6-0PT and was originally built in 1883 by Kitson of Leeds (works number 2509) for the Consett Iron Company. She is now preserved by the Tyne and Wear County Council.

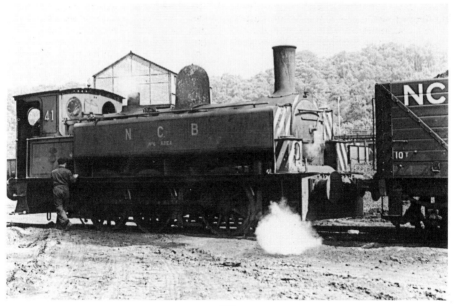

FURTHER READING

Bennett, A. Rosling. *The Chronicles of Boulton's Siding*. Locomotive Publishing Company, 1927; reprinted by David and Charles, 1971.

Hayes, G. *Collieries in the Manchester Coalfields*. De Archaeologische Pers, Eindhoven, Netherlands, 1987.

Hutchinson, Ian K. *Traction Engine Locomotives*. The Road Locomotive Society, 1981.

Industrial Locomotive Society. *Steam Locomotives in Industry*. David and Charles, 1967.

Industrial Railway Record. Journal of the Industrial Railway Society, 2 Garrick Gardens, Sholing, Southampton.

Mountford, Colin E. *The Bowes Railway*. Industrial Railway Society and Tyne and Wear Industrial Monuments Trust, 1976.

Peaty, Ian F. *Brewery Railways*. David and Charles, 1985.

Thorp, Don. *The Railways of the Manchester Ship Canal*. Oxford Publishing Company, Poole, Dorset, 1984.

Tonks, Eric S. *Ironstone Railways and Tramways of the Midlands*. Locomotive Publishing Company, 1959. Reissued by Runpast Publishing, 1988.

Wear, Russell. *Locomotive Builders of Kilmarnock*. Industrial Railway Society.

Wear, Russell, and Lees, Eric. *Stephen Lewin and the Poole Foundry*. Industrial Railway Society and Industrial Locomotive Society, 1978.

PLACES TO VISIT

Many of the locations listed are operated entirely by volunteers. The hours of opening to the public may be restricted to weekends or to certain weekends in the year. Locations where locomotives are regularly operated are marked with an asterisk. The list is not exhaustive and locomotives displayed in public parks on plinths have been generally omitted.

ENGLAND
Alderney Railway Society, Mannez Quarry, Alderney, Channel Islands. Telephone: 048182 3457.*
Bicton Woodland Railway, East Budleigh, Budleigh Salterton, Devon. Telephone: 0395 68465.*
Birmingham Railway Museum, The Steam Depot, Warwick Road, Tyseley, Birmingham. Telephone: 021-707 4696.*
Bitton Steam Centre, Bitton Station, Bristol. Telephone: 0272 327296.*
Bluebell Railway, Sheffield Park Station, near Uckfield, East Sussex. Telephone: 082572 2370.*
Bodmin and Wenford Railway, Bodmin General Station, Cornwall. Telephone: 0208 77963.*
Bowes Railway, Springwell, Tyne and Wear. Telephone: 091416 6956.*
Bradford Industrial Museum, Moorside Mill, Moorside Road, Eccleshill, Bradford, West Yorkshire. Telephone: 0274 631756.
Bressingham Gardens and Live Steam Museum, Diss, Norfolk. Telephone: 037988 386.*
Bristol Industrial Museum, Princes Wharf, Bristol. Telephone: 0272 299771.*
Buckfastleigh and Totnes Steam Railway, Buckfastleigh, Devon. Telephone: 0364 42338.*
Buckinghamshire Railway Centre, Quainton Road Station, near Aylesbury. Telephone: 0296 75450.*
Bulmer Railway Centre, Moorfields, Hereford. Telephone: 0272 834430.*
Cadeby Light Railway, The Old Rectory, Cadeby, Market Bosworth, Leicestershire. Telephone: 0455 290462.*
Cambrian Railways Society, Oswestry Station, Shropshire. Telephone: 0691 661648.
Chalk Pits Museum, Amberley, West Sussex. Telephone: 0798 831370.*
Chasewater Light Railway, Norton Canes, near Cannock, Staffordshire. Telephone: 0543 452623.*
Chatterley Whitfield Mining Museum, Tunstall, Stoke-on-Trent, Staffordshire. Telephone: 0782 813337.*
Colne Valley Railway, Castle Hedingham, Halstead, Essex. Telephone: 0787 61174.*
Cornish Steam Locomotive Society, Imperial Kiln, Bugle, near St Austell, Cornwall.
Darlington (North Road Station) Railway Museum, County Durham. Telephone: 0325 460532.
Dean Forest Railway, Norchard, near Lydney, Gloucestershire. Telephone: 0594 43423.*
Didcot Railway Centre, Didcot, Oxfordshire. Telephone: 0235 817200.*
Dinting Railway Centre, Dinting, near Glossop, Derbyshire. Telephone: 04574 5596.*

Dover Transport Museum, Dover Pumping Station, Connaught Road, Dover, Kent. Telephone: 0304 208226.

East Lancashire Railway, Castlecroft Road, Bury, Greater Manchester. Telephone: 061-764 7790.*

East Somerset Railway, West Cranmore Station, near Shepton Mallet, Somerset. Telephone: 074988 417.*

Embsay Steam Railway, Embsay Station, near Skipton, North Yorkshire Telephone: 0756 4727.*

Foxfield Light Railway, Blythe Bridge, near Stoke-on-Trent, Staffordshire. Telephone: 0782 314532.*

Gloucestershire Warwickshire Railway, Toddington Station, Cheltenham, Gloucestershire. Telephone: 024269 346.*

Great Central Railway, Loughborough, Leicestershire. Telephone: 0509 230726.*

Greater Manchester Museum of Science and Industry, Liverpool Road, Manchester. Telephone: 061-832 2244.*

Hollycombe Steam and Woodland Garden Society, Ironhill, Liphook, Hampshire. Telephone: 0428 724900.*

Ironbridge Gorge Museum Trust, Coalbrookdale Museum, Telford, Shropshire. Telephone: 095245 3522.

Isle of Wight Steam Railway, Haven Street Station, near Ryde, Isle of Wight. Telephone: 0428 724900.*

Keighley and Worth Valley Railway, Oxenhope Station, near Keighley, West Yorkshire. Telephone: 0535 45214.*

Kent and East Sussex Railway, Tenterden, Kent. Telephone: 05806 2943.*

Lakeside and Haverthwaite Railway, Haverthwaite, Ulverston, Cumbria. Telephone: 0448 31594.*

Launceston Steam Railway, St Thomas Road, Launceston, Cornwall. Telephone: 0566 5665.*

Leeds Industrial Museum, Armley Mill, Leeds, West Yorkshire. Telephone: 0532 637862.*

Leighton Buzzard Narrow Gauge Railway, Pages Park, Leighton Buzzard, Bedfordshire. Telephone: 0525 373888.*

Liverpool Museum, William Brown Street, Liverpool. Telephone: 051-207 0001.

London Transport Museum, Covent Garden, London WC2. Telephone: 01-379 6344.

Market Bosworth Light Railway (Battlefield Line), Shackerstone, Leicestershire. Telephone: 0827 880754.*

Middleton Railway, Tunstall Road, Hunslet, Leeds, West Yorkshire. Telephone: 0532 710320.*

Mid-Hants Railway, Alresford Station, Hampshire. Telephone: 096273 4200.

Midland Railway Centre, Butterley Station, Ripley, Derbyshire. Telephone: 0773 47674.*

Museum of Army Transport, Beverley, North Humberside. Telephone: 0482 860445.

Museum of Science and Industry, Newhall Street, Birmingham. Telephone: 021-236 1022.

National Railway Museum, Leeman Road, York. Telephone: 0904 21261.

Nene Valley Railway, Wansford and Peterborough, Cambridgeshire. Telephone: 0780 782921.*

Northampton Ironstone Railway Trust, Hunsbury Hill, Northampton. Telephone: 0604 498550.*

North Downs Steam Railway, Stone Lodge, Dartford, Kent. Telephone: 0634 61879.*

North Norfolk Railway, Sheringham, Norfolk. Telephone: 0263 822045.*

North of England Open Air Museum, Beamish, Stanley, County Durham. Telephone: 0207 860728.*

North Woolwich Old Station Museum, Pier Road, North Woolwich, London E16 2JJ. Telephone: 01-474 7244.

North Yorkshire Moors Railway, Grosmont, Whitby, North Yorkshire. Telephone: 0751 72508.*

Peak Railway, Buxton, Derbyshire. Telephone: 0298 79898.*

Rutland Railway Museum, Cottesmore, near Oakham, Leicestershire. Telephone: 0780 62384 and 0572 813203.*

St Austell China Clay Museum, Wheal Martyn, St Austell, Cornwall. Telephone: 0726 850362.

Saltram House, Plympton, Plymouth, Devon. Telephone: 0752 336546 and 342252.

Science Museum, Exhibition Road, London SW7 2DD. Telephone: 01-589 3456.

Severn Valley Railway, Bridgnorth, Shropshire. Telephone: 0299 403816.*

Sittingbourne and Kemsley Light Railway, Sittingbourne, Kent. Telephone: 0634 32320.*

Steamport, Derby Road, Southport, Merseyside. Telephone: 0704 30693.*

Steamtown, Warton Road, Carnforth, Lancashire. Telephone: 0524 732100.*

Stephenson Museum Project, Middle Engine Lane, West Chirton, North Shields, Tyne and Wear. Telephone: 091-232 6789.*

Stour Valley Railway, Chappel and Wakes Colne Station, Colchester, Essex. Telephone: 07875 2571.*

Swanage Railway, Swanage Station, Dorset. Telephone: 0929 425800.*

Swindon and Cricklade Railway, Blunsdon Station, near Swindon, Wiltshire. Telephone: 0793 721252.*

Tanfield Railway, Marley Hill, Newcastle upon Tyne. Telephone: 091-274 2002.*

Telford Steam Trust, Old Locomotive Shed, Horsehay, Telford, Shropshire. Telephone: 0952 49753 and 503880.*

Thursford Steam and Organ Museum, Thursford, near Fakenham, Norfolk. Telephone: 0328 3839.*

West Lancashire Light Railway, Hesketh Bank, near Preston, Lancashire. Telephone: 0942 218078.*

West Somerset Railway, S & D Railway Trust, Washford Station, Watchet, Somerset. Telephone: 0643 4996.

Whipsnade and Umfozoli Railway, Whipsnade Zoo, Dunstable, Bedfordshire. Telephone: 0582 872171.*

WALES

Brecon Mountain Railway, Pant Station, near Merthyr Tydfil, Mid Glamorgan. Telephone: 0685 4854.*

Caerphilly Railway Society, Harold Wilson Industrial Estate, Van Road, Caerphilly, Mid Glamorgan. Telephone: 0633 273182.

Gwili Railway, Bronwydd Arms, near Carmarthen, Dyfed. Telephone: 0656 732176.*

Industrial Railway Museum, Penrhyn Castle, near Bangor, Gwynedd. Telephone: 0248 353084.

Kidwelly Industrial Museum, Llangadog, Kidwelly, Dyfed. Telephone: 0554 891078.

Llangollen Railway, Llangollen, Clwyd. Telephone: 0978 860951.*

Narrow Gauge Railway Centre, Gloddfa Ganol, Blaenau Ffestiniog, Gwynedd. Telephone: 0766 830704.

Pontypool and Blaenafon Railway, Big Pit, Blaenafon, Gwent. Telephone: 0495 790311.*

Rheilffordd Llyn Padarn/Llanberis Lake Railway, Llanberis, Gwynedd. Telephone: 0286 870549.*

Rheilffordd Llyn Tegid/Bala Lake Railway, Llanuwchllyn, Bala, Gwynedd. Telephone: 06784 666.*

Rheilffordd Ysgafn Ucheldir Cymru/Welsh Highland Light Railway, Porthmadog, Gwynedd. Telephone: 051327 3576.*

Swansea Vale Railway Preservation Society, Six Pit Junction, Llansamlet, West Glamorgan.

Talyllyn Railway, Tywyn, Gwynedd. Telephone: 0654 710472.*

Welsh Industrial and Maritime Museum, Bute Street, Cardiff. Telephone: 0222 481919.

Welshpool and Llanfair Light Railway, Llanfair Caereinion, Welshpool, Powys. Telephone: 0938 810441.*

SCOTLAND

Bo'ness and Kinneil Railway, Union Street, Bo'ness, West Lothian. Telephone: 0506 822298.*

Caledonian Railway, Brechin Station, Angus, Tayside. Telephone: 03562 4562.*

Lochty Private Railway, near Anstruther, Fife. Telephone: 0592 264587.*

Pittencrieff Park, Dunfermline, Fife. (Locomotive on plinth.)

Royal Museum of Scotland, Chambers Street, Edinburgh. Telephone: 031-225 7534.

Scottish Industrial Railway Centre, Minnivey Colliery, Dalmellington, Ayrshire, Strathclyde. Telephone: 0292 313149.*

Scottish Mining Museum, Prestongrange, East Lothian EH32 9RX. Telephone: 031-665 9904.

Strathspey Railway, Boat of Garten Station, Inverness-shire, Highland. Telephone: 047983 692.*

Summerlee Heritage Museum, Coatbridge, Lanarkshire, Strathclyde. Telephone: 0236 31261.

IRELAND

Belfast and County Down Railway Trust, Downpatrick, County Down.

The Guinness Museum, The Old Hopstore, Dublin 8.

Irish Steam Preservation Society, Main Street, Stradbally, County Laois. Telephone: 010-353 502 25136.

Railway Preservation Society, Whitehead, Carrickfergus, County Antrim. Telephone: 09603 78567.*

Shanes Castle, Randalstown, County Antrim. Telephone: 084941 2216.*

Ulster Folk and Transport Museum, Witham Street, Belfast. Telephone: 0232 451519.

Ulster Folk and Transport Museum, Cultra Manor, Holywood, County Down. Telephone: 0232 451519.*